THE ESSENCE OF

ZEN

THE ESSENCE OF

ZEN

An Anthology of Quotations

Compiled by *Maggie Pinkney*

THE FIVE MILE PRESS

The Five Mile Press

The Five Mile Press Pty Ltd
950 Stud Road, Rowville
Victoria 3178
Australia

Email: publishing@fivemile.com.au
Website: www.fivemile.com.au

First published 2005

Designed by Zoë Murphy
Printed in China

National Library of Australia Cataloguing in Publication

The essence of Zen: an anthology of quotations

ISBN 1 74124 762 4

Zen Buddhism – Quotations, maxims, etc. I. Pinkney, Maggie.

294.3927

CONTENTS

INTRODUCTION

Zen is about standing back, letting go – and getting in touch with the peace and wisdom that lies within us all. It's about the discovery of the sacred in the midst of the humble and ordinary. About not getting caught up in the rat-race and the endless search for material possessions.

With its emphasis on looking within, enjoying the moment, detachment and compassion, Zen offers a refreshingly different slant on life. To experience Zen is a bit like looking through the other end of the telescope.

Meditation, as practised by Buddha, and brought to Japan by the twelfth-century monk Dogen, is at the heart of Zen.

In fact, the word 'Zen' is Japanese for meditation as well as for the school of philosophy surrounding it. However, it is not necessary to be a serious practitioner of Zen to benefit from the collected wisdom of this anthology. Gathered from a wide range of sources, from ancient Zen masters to modern American Zen followers – and poets, philosophers and writers from many other nations – these quotations provide insights that give a fresh new perspective to us all, and can be incorporated into our thinking, regardless of our religion or culture.

The inspirational thoughts contained in this book will help you to see life through 'Zen eyes', freeing you from fruitless regrets, desires and anxieties – and helping you to appreciate every moment of your life on earth.

Maggie Pinkney, 2005

THE ESSENCE OF ZEN

Zen in its essence

is the art of seeing

into the nature of one's being,

and it points the way

from bondage to freedom.

D.T. SUZUKI

Outside teaching; apart from tradition.

Not founded on words and letters.

Pointing directly to the human mind.

Seeing into one's nature and attaining
Buddhahood.

Walking is Zen, sitting is Zen.

Whether talking or remaining silent,

Whether moving or standing quiet,

The Essence itself is ever at ease.

DAISHI

Refraining from all evil,

not clinging to birth and death,

working in deep compassion

for all sentient beings,

respecting those over you

and pitying those below you,

without any detesting or desiring,

worrying or lamentation –

this is what is called Buddha.

Do not search beyond it.

———————

DOGEN

Calm in quietude is not real calm.

When you can be calm in the midst of activity,

this is the true state of nature.

Happiness in comfort is not real happiness.

When you can be happy

in the midst of hardship,

then you see the true potential of

the mind.

HUANCHU DAOREN

Do not seek the truth.

Only cease to cherish opinions.

———————

ZEN SAYING

A primary aim of Zen

is the uncovering of what is known

as inherent knowledge ... It is said that

the ignorant are obstructed by ignorance,

while intellectuals are obstructed

by intellectual knowledge.

One way of getting past these obstacles

and approaching inherent knowledge

is to let go of whatever comes to mind.

MUSO KOKUSHI

Zen mind is not Zen mind.

That is, if you are attached to Zen mind,

then you have a problem,

and your way is very narrow.

Throwing away Zen mind is correct Zen mind.

Only keep the question,

'What is the best way of helping other people?'

SEUNG SAHN

One who excels in traveling
leaves no wheel tracks.
One who excels as a warrior
does not appear formidable.
One who excels in fighting
is never aroused in anger.
One who excels in defeating his enemy
does not join issue.
One who excels in employing others
humbles himself before them.

ZEN TRADITION

LOOK TO THIS
DAY

Look to this day.

In it lie all the realities and verities of existence,

the bliss of growth, the splendor of action,

the glory of power.

For yesterday is but a dream and

tomorrow is only a vision.

But today, well-lived, makes every yesterday

a dream of happiness and every tomorrow

a vision of hope.

SANSKRIT PROVERB

Each soul must meet

the morning sun,

the new sweet earth,

and the Great Silence.

OHIYESHA (CHARLES ALEXANDER EASTMAN)

An inch of time is an inch of gold: treasure it.

Appreciate its fleeting nature;

misplaced gold is easily found,

misspent time is lost forever.

LOY CHING-YUEN

Past and future are illusions.

They exist only in the present,

which is what there is

and all that there is.

ALAN WATTS

To see a World in a grain of Sand

And a heaven in a Wild Flower,

Hold Infinity in the palm of your hand

And Eternity in an hour.

WILLIAM BLAKE

When I begin to sit
with the dawn in solitude,
I begin to really live.
It makes me treasure
every single moment of life.

GLORIA VANDERBILT

Nothing is worth more
than this day.

JOHANN VON GOETHE

Ask not what tomorrow may bring,

but count as blessing

every day that Fate allows you.

HORACE

Do not dwell in the past.

Do not dream of the future.

Concentrate the mind

on the present moment.

BUDDHA

You have to live on this earth

twenty-four hours of daily time.

Out of it you have to spin health, pleasure,

money, content, respect and

the evolution of your immortal soul.

Its right use, most effective use,

is a matter of the highest urgency

and of the most thrilling actuality.

All depends on that.

We shall never have any more time.

ARNOLD BENNETT

He who binds to himself a joy,

Does the winged life destroy;

But he who kisses joy as it flies

Lives in Eternity's sunrise.

WILLIAM BLAKE

Happy the man, and happy he alone,

He who can call today his own:

He who, secure within, can say

Tomorrow do thy worst,

for I have lived today.

JOHN DRYDEN

O gift of God! a perfect day,

Whereon no man should work but play,

Whereon it is enough for me,

Not to be doing but to be.

HENRY WADSWORTH LONGFELLOW

A lifetime is not what's between
The moments of birth and death.
A lifetime is one moment
Between my two little breaths.
The present, the here, the now,
That's all the life I get,
I live each moment in full,
In kindness, in peace, without regret.

CHADE MENG

We are here and it is now.

Further than that,

all human knowledge

is moonshine.

H.L. MENCKEN

Write in your heart

that every day

is the best day of the year.

RALPH WALDO EMERSON

As yesterday is history

and tomorrow may never come,

I have resolved from this day on,

I will do all the business I can honestly,

have all the fun I can reasonably,

do all the good I can do willingly,

and save my digestion by

thinking pleasantly.

ROBERT LOUIS STEVENSON

When you arise in the morning

Give thanks for the morning light.

Give thanks for your life and strength.

Give thanks for your food.

And give thanks for the joy of living.

And if perchance you see

no reason to give thanks

Rest assured the fault is yours.

AMERICAN INDIAN SAYING

To see the things of the present moment

is to see all that is now,

all that has been since time began,

and all that shall be unto the world's end;

for all things are of

one kind and one form.

MARCUS AURELIUS

Out of Eternity

the new Day is born;

Into Eternity at night will return.

THOMAS CARLYLE

EVERYDAY ZEN

Sit

Rest

Work.

Alone with yourself,

Never weary.

On the edge of the forest

Live joyfully,

Without desire.

———————————

BUDDHA

There is no place in Buddhism

for using effort.

Just be ordinary and nothing special.

Relieve your bowels, pass water,

Put on your clothes and eat your food.

When you're tired, go and lie down.

Ignorant people will laugh at me,

But the wise will understand.

LIN-CHI

Each morning sees some task begun,

Each evening sees it close.

Something attempted, something done,

Has earned a night's repose.

———————————

HENRY WADSWORTH LONGFELLOW

I got up at sunrise and was happy,
I walked, and was happy;
I roamed the forests and hills,
I wandered in the valleys,
I read. I did nothing,
I worked in the garden,
I picked fruit,

I helped in the house and happiness

followed me everywhere —

happiness which could not be referred

to any definite object,

but dwelt entirely within myself

and which never left me a single instant.

JEAN-JAQUES ROUSSEAU

There are two ways to live your life.

One is as though nothing is a miracle.

The other is as though everything

is a miracle.

ALBERT EINSTEIN

There are

no mundane things outside of Buddhism,

and there is

no Buddhism outside of mundane things.

———————

YUAN-WU

Either hoeing the garden

or washing bottles at the well,

making soup for a sick man

or listening to someone else's child,

studying books, stacking logs,

writing to the local paper

or pulling that stubborn lamb into our world,

I hear the song which carried my neighbor

from one thing to the next:

Earth feeds us out of her empty bowl.

PETER LEVITT

Teach us delight in

simple things.

RUDYARD KIPLING

To have some deep feeling about Buddhism

is not the point;

we just do what we should do,

like eating supper and going to bed.

This is Buddhism!

SUZUKI ROSHI

Washing dishes

is not only a Zen exercise,

but you get the dishes

clean too.

ROBERT ALLEN

The secret of seeing things as they are

is to take off our colored spectacles.

That being-as-it-is,

with nothing extraordinary about it,

nothing wonderful, is the great wonder.

The ability to see things normally

is no small thing;

to be really normal is the unusual.

In that normality begins to bubble up

inspiration.

SESSAN

The miracle

is not to fly in the air,

or to walk on the water:

but to walk on the earth.

CHINESE PROVERB

Zen is an exploration of reality.

It is about your life in the place

where you live, Here and Now.

It is this immediacy

that gives it its strength.

I drink tea

and forget the world's noises.

CHINESE SAYING

The first cup moistens my lips and throat,

The second cup breaks my loneliness,

The third cup searches my inmost being …

The fourth cup raises a slight perspiration –

All the wrongs of life

pass away through my pores.

At the fifth cup I am purified;

The sixth cup calls me

to the realms of immortals.

The seventh cup – ah,

but I could take no more!

I only feel the breath

of cool wind that rises in my sleeves.

Where is Heaven?

Let me ride on this sweet breeze

and waft away thither.

CHINESE POEM

What a delight it is

When I blow away the ash,

To watch the crimson

Of the glowing fire

And hear the water boil.

TACHIBANA AKEMI

Zen

is not some kind of excitement,

but merely concentration

on our usual everyday routine.

SHRUNKYU SUZUKI

Take Ten

Arranging a bowl of flowers in the morning

can give a sense of quiet to a crowded day –

like writing a poem or saying a prayer.

What matters is that one be for a time

inwardly attentive.

ANNE MORROW LINDBERGH

The quieter you become

The more you are able

to hear.

ZEN SAYING

The most valuable thing

we can do for the psyche, occasionally,

is to let it rest, wander,

live in the changing light of a room,

not try to be or do

anything whatever.

—————————

MAY SARTON

Within yourself

is a stillness and a sanctuary

to which you can retreat at any time

and be yourself.

HERMANN HESSE

Solitude is freedom.

It's an anchor, an anchor in the void.

You're anchored to nothing,

and that's my definition of freedom.

————————————

JOHN LILLY

There is a silence

into which the world cannot intrude.

There is an ancient peace

you carry in your heart

and have not lost.

A COURSE IN MIRACLES

Silence is a friend
who will never betray.

CONFUCIUS

Let us not therefore

go hurrying about

and collecting honey, bee-like,

buzzing here and there impatiently

from a knowledge of what is to be arrived at.

But let us open our leaves like a flower,

and be passive and receptive.

JOHN KEATS

Meditating deeply ...

reach the depth of the source.

Branching streams

cannot compare to this source!

Sitting alone in a great silence,

even though the heavens turn

and the earth is upset,

you will not even wink.

NYOGEN SENZAKI

I was utterly alone

with the sun and the earth.

Lying down on the grass,

I spoke in my soul to the earth,

the sun, the air,

and the distant sea ...

RICHARD JEFFRIES

I am sure of this,

that by going much alone

a man will get more

of a noble courage in thought and word

than from all the wisdom

in books.

RALPH WALDO EMERSON

Bitter rain soaks the pile of kindling twigs.

The night so cold and still the lamp flame

hardly moves.

Clouds condense and drench our stone

walled hut.

Broken rushes clog the reed gate's way.

The stream gurgles, a torrent in its bed.

That's all we hear. Only rarely comes a
   human voice.
But oh, how priceless is this peace of mind
   that fills us
As we sit on our heels and put on another
   Chan monk's robe!

———————

HSU YUN

Training began with children,

who were taught to sit still and enjoy it.

They were taught to use their organs of smell,

to look where there was

apparently nothing to see,

and to listen intently

when all seemingly was quiet.

CHIEF STANDING BEAR

Sit quietly doing nothing,

spring comes,

and the grass grows

by itself.

ZEN WISDOM

You do not need to leave your room.

Remain sitting at your table and listen.

Do not even listen, simply wait.

Do not even wait, be still and solitary.

The world will freely offer itself to you

to be unmasked, it has no choice.

It will roll in ecstasy at your feet.

FRANZ KAFKA

The goal of a healthy solitude is love;

love and acceptance of ourselves as we are

and where we are,

and love and compassion for others.

DOROTHY PAYNE

When man sits,

then the coarse passions subside and

the luminous mind arises in awareness:

Thus consciousness is illuminated.

MEISTER ECKHART

Settle in solitude,

and you will come upon Him

in yourself.

ST. TERESA

Pearls lie not on the seashore.

If thou desirest one

thou must dive for it.

CHINESE SAYING

So it is that every spiritual healing

is the result of one individual sitting

in the Silence, quietly, peacefully waiting,

and then the Spirit comes

through the consciousness of that one –

the voice thunders in the Silence,

and the Earth melts.

JOEL S. GOLDSMITH

The foolish reject what they see;

The wise reject what they think.

ZEN SAYING

What is this life, if

Full of care,

We have no time

To stand and stare?

———————

W. H. DAVIES

This is what is strange –
that friends, even passionate love,
are not my real life unless
there is time alone in which to discover
what is happening
or has happened.

———————

MAY SARTON

Teach us to care

and not to care.

Teach us to sit still.

T. S. ELIOT

We must, like a painter,

take time to stand back from our work,

to be still, and thus see what's what …

True repose is standing back to survey

the activities that fill our lives.

WILLIAM MCNAMARA

Praying is not about asking;

it's about listening ...

It is just opening your eyes to see

what was there all along.

CHAGDUD TULKU RINPOCHE

My home is

my retreat and resting place from the wars.

I try to keep this corner

as a haven against the tempest outside,

as I do another corner of my soul.

MICHEL DE MONTAIGNE

Your vision will become clear only

when you can look into your heart.

Who looks outside, dreams.

Who looks inside, awakes.

———————

CARL JUNG

Truth is within ourselves; it takes no rise

From outward things, what'er you may believe.

There is an inmost centre in us all,

Where truth abides in fullness.

ROBERT BROWNING

THE ZEN OF CHANGE

Love not what you are

but what you may become.

MIGUEL DE CERVANTES

Be not afraid of growing slowly.

Be afraid of standing still.

CHINESE PROVERB

The purpose of life is to live it,

to taste experience to the utmost,

to reach out eagerly and without fear

for newer and richer experience.

ELEANOR ROOSEVELT

Only in growth, reform and change,

paradoxically enough,

is true security to be found.

———————

ANNE MORROW LINDBERGH

If our nature is permitted to guide our life,
we grow healthy, fruitful and happy.

ABRAHAM MASLOW

Life is change.

Growth is optional.

Choose wisely.

KAREN KAISER CLARK

My business is not to remake myself,

But make the absolute best

of what God made.

ROBERT BROWNING

I think these difficult times
have helped me to understand better
than before how infinitely rich and
beautiful life is in every way,
and that so many things
one goes around worrying about
are of no importance whatever.

ISAK DINESEN (KAREN BLIXEN)

We deem those happy

who from the experience of life

have learned to bear its ills

without being overcome by them.

———————

CARL JUNG

Examine myself as I may,

I can no longer find the slightest trace of

the anxious, agitated individual of those years,

so discontented with herself,

so out of patience with others.

———————

GEORGE SAND (AMANDINE DUPIN)

The real voyage of discovery
consists not in seeking new landscapes
but in having new eyes.

MARCEL PROUST

You must learn day by day,

year by year,

to broaden your horizons.

The more things you love,

the more you are interested in,

the more you enjoy,

the more you are indignant about –

the more you have left

if anything goes wrong.

ETHEL BARRYMORE

We shrink from change;

yet is there anything that can

come into being without it?

Change is part of nature itself.

Do you not see, then, that change in yourself

is of the same order, and no less necessary

than to Nature?

MARCUS AURELIUS

We must always change, renew, rejuvenate ourselves; otherwise we harden.

JOHANN VON GOETHE

The only way
to make sense out of change
is to plunge with it,
move with it,
and join the dance.

———————

ALAN WATTS

He who is not

satisfied with himself

will grow.

HEBREW PROVERB

Moments of guilt,

moments of contrition,

moments when we are lacking in self-esteem,

moments when we are bearing the trial

of being displeasing to ourselves,

are essential to our growth.

M. SCOTT PECK

Every small positive change

we make in ourselves

repays us in confidence

in the future.

ALICE WALKER

THE ZEN OF
NATURE

The autumn mountains

Here and there

Smoke rising

————————

GYODAI

Autumn's colors dropping from branches

in masses of falling leaves.

Cold clouds bringing rain

into the crannies of the mountains:

Everyone was born

with the same sort of eyes –

Why do mine keep seeing things

as a Zen Koan?

MUSO

Contemplating the clear moon

Reflecting a mind empty as the open sky –

Drawn by its beauty,

I lose myself

In the shadows it casts.

DOGEN

A lightning flash –

The sound of water drops

Falling through bamboo

BUSON

With plum blossom scent,

This sudden sun emerges

Along a mountain trail

BASHO

Although I try to hold the single thought

of Buddha's teaching in my heart,

I cannot help but hear the

many crickets' voices calling as well.

ISUMI SHIKIBU

The blue mountain bordering the sea

does not move,

but the mind of the bird over the waves

breaks free

and follows the course of the river.

——————

DAISHI

Village has grown old –

Not a single house without

Persimmon trees

BASHO

You ask why I make

my home in the mountain forest,

and I smile, and am silent,

and even my soul remains quiet;

it lives in the other world

which no one owns.

The peach trees blossom.

The water flows.

LI PO

Every part of this earth is sacred to my people.

Every shining pine needle,

every sandy shore.

Every mist in the dark woods,

every clearing and

every humming insect

is holy in

the memory of my people.

CHIEF SEATH
FROM A LETTER TO THE PRESIDENT OF THE USA, 1883

Love all God's creations,

both the whole and every grain of sand.

Love every leaf, every ray of light.

Love the animals, love the plants,

love each separate thing.

If thou love each thing

thou wilt perceive the mystery

of God in all ...

FEODOR DOSTOEVSKY

There is a pleasure in the pathless woods,

There is a rapture on the lonely shore,

There is society, where none intrudes,

By the deep Sea, and music in its roar.

I love not Man the less, but Nature more.

LORD BYRON

The thunderstorm breaks up,

One tree lit by setting sun,

A cicada cry

———————

SHIKI

Along the mountain road

Somehow it tugs at my heart

A wild violet

———

BASHO

Lighting the candles

In the thatched temple

Plum blossoms fall

———————

GYODAI

I am one

Who eats his breakfast,

Gazing at the morning-glories.

BASHO

Come forth into the light of things,

Let nature be your teacher.

———————

WILLIAM WORDSWORTH

Like the little stream

Making its way through the mossy crevices

I, too, quietly

Turn clear and transparent.

The wind has settled, the blossoms have fallen;

Birds sing, the mountains grow dark –

Thus is the wondrous power of Buddhism.

———————

RYOKAN

Chilling autumn rains

Curtain Mount Fuji, then make it

More beautiful to see

BASHO

Gentle as a dead friend's hand

Resting on my shoulder

This autumn sunshine

———————

KUSADAO

Evening bell:

Persimmons pelt

The temple garden

———————

SHIKI

Under this tree, where light and shade

Speckle the grass like a Thrush's breast,

Here, in this green and quiet place,

I give myself to peace and rest.

W. H. DAVIS

On that far mountain

On the slope below the peak,

Cherries are in flower.

Oh, let the mountain mists

Not arise to hide the scene.

———————

OE NO MASAFUSA

If only I could share it:

The soft sound of snow

Falling late at night

At this old temple.

HAKUIN

If your hermitage

Is deep in the mountains

Surely the moon,

Flowers and crimson leaves

Will become your friends.

Wild peonies

Now at their peak in glorious full bloom:

Too precious to pick

Too precious not to pick.

RYOKEN

Dozing on horseback

Smoke from the tea-fires

Drifts to the moon

——————

BASHO

THE
GREAT ONENESS

Earth, mountains, rivers – hidden in
this nothingness.
In the nothingness – earth, mountains,
rivers revealed.
Spring flowers, winter snows:
There's no being or non-being, nor
denial itself.

SAISHO

The One and the All.

Mingle and move without discriminating.

Live in this awareness and you'll stop worrying

about not being perfect.

SENG T'SAN

I believe God is everything …

Everything that is or ever was or ever will be.

And when you can feel that,

and be happy to feel that, you've found it …

My first step from the old white man was trees.

Then air. Then birds. Then other people.

But one day when I was sitting quiet

and feeling like a motherless child,

which I was, it came to me:

that feeling of being part of everything,

not separate at all.

I knew that if I cut a tree,

my arm would bleed.

And I laughed and I cried

and I ran all round the house.

I knew just what it was.

In fact, when it happens,

you can't miss it.

ALICE WALKER *The Color Purple*

It is as if

a raindrop fell from heaven

into a stream or fountain

and became one with the water in it

so that never again can the raindrop

be separated from the water of the stream;

or as if a little brook ran into the sea

and there was thenceforward no means

of distinguishing its water from the ocean;

or as if a brilliant light came into a room

through two windows and though it

comes in divided between them,

it forms a single light inside.

ST. TERESA

How can the drops of water

Know themselves to be a river?

ZEN SAYING

You are Brahman,

I am Brahman,

the whole universe is Brahman.

Whatever you are doing,

realise this truth at all times.

This Brahman or the self alone

is the reality in all beings,

even as clay is the real substance

in thousands of pots.

HINDU WISDOM

Above, below and around you, all is

Spontaneously existing, for

There is nowhere which is

Outside Buddha-Mind.

HUANG PO

Thirty spokes join together in the hub.

It is because of what is not there

that the cart is useful.

Clay is formed into a vessel.

It is because of its emptiness

that the vessel is useful.

Cut doors and windows to make a room.

It is because of its emptiness

that the room is useful.

Therefore, what is present is used for profit.

But it is in absence that there is usefulness.

LAO-TZU

Death,

like birth,

is one of Nature's secrets;

the same elements that have been combined

are then dispersed ... For being endowed

with mind it is no anomaly,

nor in any way inconsistent

with the plan of their creation.

MARCUS AURELIUS

In darkness light exists,

do not look with a dark view.

In light darkness exists,

do not look with a luminous view.

Light and darkness create an opposition,

Yet depend on each other just as the step

Taken by the right leg depends on the step

Taken by the left.

SEKITO

Where beauty is,

then there is ugliness;

where right is, also there is wrong.

Knowledge and ignorance are interdependent;

delusion and enlightenment

condition each other.

Since olden times it has been so.

How could it be otherwise now?

———————————

RYOKAN

All beings by nature are Buddha,

as ice by nature is water;

apart from water there is no ice,

apart from beings,

no Buddha.

───────────

HAKUIN

ZEN
ENLIGHTENMENT

He who loves

does not think about his own life;

to love truly,

a man must forget about himself.

If your desires do not accord with your spirit,

sacrifice them,

and you will come to the end of your journey.

If the body of desire obstructs the way,

reject it; then fix your eyes

in front and contemplate.

ATTAR

A luminous moon,

the wind in the pine,

a long evening,

a transcendent view:

but what is the meaning of this?

What is the meaning of life?

Value judgments are destructive

to our proper business,

which is curiosity

and awareness.

JOHN CAGE

I see people in the world
Throw away their lives lusting after things,
Never able to satisfy their desires,
Falling into deep despair
And torturing themselves.
Even if they get what they want
How long will they be able to enjoy it?
For one heavenly pleasure
They suffer ten torments of hell,
Binding themselves more firmly
to the grindstone.

Such people are like monkeys

Frantically grasping for the moon in the water

And then falling into a whirlpool.

How endlessly those caught up

in the floating world

Suffer.

RYOKAN

Keep your heart clear and transparent

And you will never be bound.

A single disturbed thought,

Creates ten thousand distractions.

Let myriad things captivate you

And you'll go further and further astray.

How painful to see people

All wrapped up in themselves.

———————

RYOKAN

To get rid of your passions

is not nirvana –

to look upon them as no matter of yours,

that is nirvana.

———————

ZEN SAYING

As for the people and affairs
of the contemporary world,
they hold no attraction for me.
If in becoming a teacher one thinks only
of wealth and honor and is not concerned
about the importance of literature,
it would be better if we had no teachers.
If in being a friend one thinks only
of power and profit and cares nothing
about the frank exchange of opinions,
it would be better if we had no friends.

So I close my gate,

shut my door,

hum poems

and sing songs

by myself.

———————

YOSHISHIGE NO YATSUTANE

If your house

is your most important possession

then it is your prison.

Your house should be

a hostel you stay in

day after day.

ROBERT ALLEN

Attraction and aversion are two feelings
that keep people within the bondage
of ignorant repetitive behavior …
If people do not crave to be pleased,
they will not be displeased.
What causes mental suffering
is not the environment
but the mind itself.

MUSO KOKUSHI

He who knows
he has enough
is rich.

LAO-TZU

It is not the body,

not the personality that is the true self.

The true self is eternal.

Even on the point of death

we can say to ourselves,

'My true self is free.

I cannot be contained'.

MARCUS AURELIUS

The true value of a human being
can be found in the degree
to which he has attained
liberation from the self.

ALBERT EINSTEIN

He who wherever he goes is attached

to no person and to no place by ties of flesh;

who accepts good and evil alike,

neither welcoming the one

nor shrinking from the other –

take it that such a one has attained

Perfection.

BHAGAVAD-GITA

Beyond the white clouds

a blue mountain.

A traveler goes

beyond that mountain.

———————

ZEN SAYING

To attain Buddhahood

we must scatter

life's aims and objects

to the winds.

ZEN TRADITION

There is no path

that leads to Zen.

How can you follow a path

to where you are

right now?

ROBERT ALLEN

It is not that I do not wish
To mix with others
But living alone in freedom
Is a better path for me.

When I think about the misery
Of those in this world,
Their sadness becomes mine.

Oh, that my monk's robe

Was wide enough

To gather up all

The suffering people

In this floating world.

RYOKAN

You wander from room to room

Hunting for the diamond necklace

That is already around your neck!

———————

RUMI

There is no beginning to practice

Nor end to enlightenment;

There is no beginning to enlightenment

Nor end to practice.

———————

DOGEN

Three things are essential:

great doubt,

great faith, and

great perseverance.

ZEN SAYING

Be soft in your practice.

Think of the method as a fine silvery stream,

not a raging waterfall.

Follow the stream, have faith in its course.

It will go its own way,

meandering here, trickling there.

It will find the grooves, the cracks, the crevices.

Just follow it.

Never let it out of your sight.

It will take you.

SHENG-YEN

The Perfect Way knows no difficulties

Except that it refuses to make preferences;

Only when freed from hate and love,

It reveals itself fully and without disguise.

———————

SOSAN

The mind is very difficult to see,

Very delicate and subtle;

It moves and lands wherever it pleases.

The wise one should guard his mind,

For a guarded mind brings happiness.

———————

DHAMMAPADA

Beneath, the mountain stream flows

On and on without end.

If one's Zen mind is like this

Seeing into one's own nature

cannot be far off.

HAKUIN

Words cannot describe everything.

The heart's message

cannot be delivered in words.

If you receive words literally you will be lost.

If you try to explain with words

you will not attain enlightenment

in this life.

MU-MON

Where there is great doubt,

there will be great awakening;

small doubt,

small awakening,

no doubt,

no awakening.

ZEN SAYING

To gain enlightenment,

you must want it

as much as a man whose head

is held under water

wants air.

ZEN SAYING

Enlightenment is like the moon

reflected on the water.

The moon does not get wet,

nor is the water broken.

Although its light is wide and great,

the moon is reflected

even in a puddle an inch wide.

The whole moon and the entire sky

are reflected in one dewdrop

on the grass.

DOGEN

Just as you see yourself in a mirror,

Form and reflection look at each other.

You are not the reflection

Yet the reflection is you.

TOSAN

In original nature

There is no this and that.

The great Round Mirror

Has no likes or dislikes.

SEUNG SAHN